Hook Norton Brewery from the yard. The visitor centre is on the right opposite the brewhouse.

Beers and Breweries
of Britain

Roger Putman

A Shire book

Published in 2004 by Shire Publications Ltd,
Cromwell House, Church Street, Princes Risborough,
Buckinghamshire HP27 9AA, UK.
(Website: www.shirebooks.co.uk)

Copyright © 2004 by Roger Putman.
First published 2004.
Shire Album 434. ISBN 0 7478 0606 3.
Roger Putman is hereby identified as the author of this
work in accordance with Section 77 of the Copyright,
Designs and Patents Act 1988.

British Library Cataloguing in Publication Data:
Putman, Roger
Beers and breweries of Britain. – (Shire album; 434)
1. Breweries – Great Britain
2. Breweries – Great Britain – Pictorial works
3. Beer – Great Britain
4. Brewing industry – Great Britain
5. Brewing industry – Great Britain – Pictorial works
I. Title 338.4'766342'0941
ISBN 0 7478 0606 3.

Cover: *(Clockwise from top left) The 1885 brick-built brewery at Wadworth in Devizes,
Wiltshire. A mechanical picker harvesting 'hedgerow' hops at Claston in Herefordshire. A
brewing copper at Highgate Brewery in Walsall. Wooden casks are becoming rare – these are at
Wadworth in Devizes.*

Back cover: *The Germans are proud of their brewing heritage. An attractive display of brewing
materials and artefacts on the Deutsches Bier stand at the Brau brewing trade show in
Nuremberg, Germany.*

ACKNOWLEDGEMENTS
The author would like to thank Diana Lay (former Curator at Coors Visitor Centre in
Burton upon Trent), Eibhlin Roche (Guinness Archive) and Ken Thomas (Scottish Courage
Archive) for helping to find old pictures. The illustrations are acknowledged as follows:
Adnams plc, page 5 (bottom); Coors Visitor Centre, Burton upon Trent, pages 29 (bottom),
36 (top); Crisp Malt, page 9; Guinness Archive, Diageo, Ireland, pages 6 (bottom), 7, 36
(bottom right), 37 (both), 40; Harveys of Lewes (from the 2003 Christmas card), page 32;
Tim O'Rourke, page 30 (all); SAB Miller, page 38; Scottish Courage Archive, pages 36
(bottom left), 53; Whitbread, from *The Brewer's Art*, page 34; Young & Co Brewery plc, page
48. All other photographs were taken by the author.

Printed in Malta by Gutenberg Press Limited, Gudja Road, Tarxien PLA 19, Malta

Contents

Introduction 4

The materials of brewing 8

The brewing process .18

The romance of beer .28

The changing face of British brewing 41

Britain's brewers today 46

Places to visit 49

Further reading 52

Some British beers to try 54

Index 56

Brass and copper of the run-off taps from the mash tun at Hook Norton Brewery near Banbury, Oxfordshire.

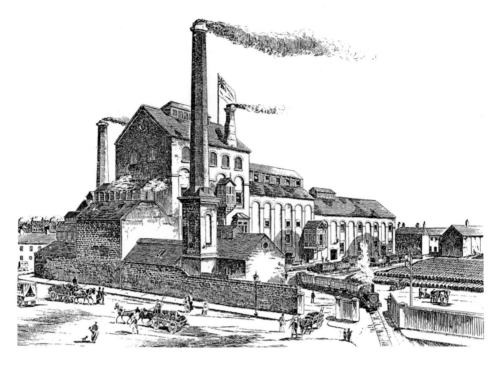

Introduction

Beer is an alcoholic beverage fermented by yeast using sugar from a cereal source. Today the cereal is mainly malted barley and beer is almost universally flavoured with hops. Beer has been known for around six thousand years and has been an integral part of the culture in many civilisations, including the British. Once upon a time the local brewery dominated the skyline in many towns in Britain, with its aroma and noise pervading the surrounding streets, but consolidation within the industry has seen over a hundred substantially sized plants close since the 1970s.

While the global brewers promote their brands, which pundits predict will take an increasing share of the British market (perhaps over three quarters by 2005), the remainder will be an eclectic mix of many revived styles.

To invigorate an interest in different beers, regional brewers have seasonal cask-ale programmes in which new beers are brought on to the market about six times a year. There are beers that use single varieties of barley and hops, wheat beers, porters, fruit beers and smoked beers, as well as the traditional winter warmer for a nightcap on those chilly evenings. There are recipes aplenty; naming the resulting beer can tax the imagination of marketing departments!

The smoking brewery stack was a common landmark in the nineteenth century. This is Eadies in Burton upon Trent from Alfred Barnard's book on 'Noted Breweries' (1890). The fermenting room on the right now houses Coors Technical Centre.

Many breweries have retained old fermenting vessels for display. These sausage-shaped wooden-clad ones with gleaming brasswork are at Adnams in Southwold, Suffolk.

Charabanc trips have been popular outings from breweries and pubs for over a century. This 1875 photograph shows the Adnams workforce off for the day.

Bateman's Brewery at Wainfleet near Skegness has incorporated a windmill into its visitor centre. The modern chimney-stack on the left is from the new brewhouse copper. Note the distinctive weathervane.

Niche beers are available in bottles as well. The Tesco Beer Challenge is held twice a year and shelf space is given to winners from the small and larger breweries. It is testimony to the success of this competition that the list of current top-twenty premium bottled-ale brands contains five past winners.

Beer is the drink of northern Europe and brewing it has been spread by mass emigration to the rest of the world. The overall world market in 2003 totalled 1478 million hectolitres, which is over 260 billion pints. Sales are generally static or declining in the developed countries. Although beer is by far the world's most popular alcoholic drink (over 70 per cent of the world's alcohol is sold as beer), in Britain, as alcohol spending reduces, the population is buying more wine. The British beer market peaked at 68 million hectolitres in 1980; two decades later it had declined by around 11 million hectolitres. Britain

Huge pyramids of wooden casks typify the size of some nineteenth-century breweries. These casks are at Guinness in Dublin. Note the 600 mm (23 inch) narrow-gauge railway.

A note on volume measurement

Traditionally the British brewer used a barrel as his main unit of volume. The barrel was 36 imperial gallons and thus 288 pints. The industry now uses the hectolitre (100 litres), which is about 22 gallons, so a barrel is just under 164 litres. A US beer barrel is smaller – only 117 litres. Hectolitres are used in this book for trading volumes, etc, but imperial volumes appear primarily where old plant is being described. A 50 barrel vessel was installed, not an 81.8 hectolitre one!

exports just 3 million hectolitres to more than 120 countries but imports over 5 million hectolitres, mainly from Germany, Ireland and the Netherlands. Britain is the world's eighth-biggest beer market, behind China, the United States, Germany, Brazil, Japan, Russia and Mexico, but it remains a market under threat.

Beer does have an image problem. In Britain it is seen as a drink of the heavy manual worker who had four pints on his way home for his supper and another four pints afterwards. Beer is downed in pints in daunting weekend evening binges; beer is associated with smoking and chips; people think it is made from chemicals, is generally unhealthy, makes you fat and is certainly not for women! Only now have the brewers decided to work together to dispel these myths and promote Britain's national range of over two thousand beer brands. Beer actually contributes to our health as well as providing a refreshing beverage to drink amongst friends.

Beer has a tremendous heritage woven into the history of Britain since pre-Roman times. Over 90 per cent of the beer consumed in Britain is brewed on home ground largely from indigenous barley and hops, and some 900,000 people directly or indirectly gain a living from the beer and pub trades. Beer contributes around £5 billion a year to the national exchequer in duty and VAT. This book aims to tell the reader more about what is undoubtedly the British 'national beverage'.

Stout has long been associated with health and as 'invalid stout' was a valuable aid to convalescence. This enamel sign from Guinness would not get past the current rules relating to advertising standards.

The materials of brewing

MALTING

Beer is more complex than wine since nature provides a ready source of fermentable sugar in the grape. In cereals the sugar that nourishes the young plant is bound up in a polymer of glucose molecules called starch. The starch needs to be broken down into glucose by the action of enzymes. It is the job of the maltster to germinate the barley and get maximum enzyme formation but with minimal growth of the young plant, which would otherwise use up potential sugar for the brewer.

Beer is made mainly from barley malt. Being low in gluten, barley makes a poor bread. The German Beer Purity Law or *Reinheitsgebot* dating from 1516 was an early attempt to ensure that valuable wheat was not diverted from baking to brewing. It was the world's first food-processing regulation. Barley grows well in a temperate climate and particularly well in a maritime one; thus British barleys yield malts that are highly sought after for the export market. Old bucolic films show peasants happily scything their way through chest-high corn. Modern varieties have short stiff straws to withstand the battering from winds; they are bred for increasing disease resistance and produce a yield that can be as high as 8 tonnes per hectare.

Barley for malting needs a low protein content. Excess protein reduces the amount of sugar available for the brewer and can encourage later hazes (cloudiness) in the beer, especially with the current trends for lower serving temperatures. Malts for cask beers that are packaged straight after fermentation should be less than 10 per cent protein while beers that are conditioned (further processed) in the brewery can be as high as 12 per cent. Farmers are paid a premium to withhold excess fertiliser to ensure lower protein levels – but this is at the expense of yield.

Good-quality malting barley grows on the lighter free-draining soils in the east of England. Bordeaux wine buffs wax lyrical about the *terroir* – the interaction between soil and microclimate; Britain has its own such condition in the barley lands of high Norfolk around Fakenham, where a 'sea fret' drifts in most afternoons in summer and keeps the barley ears from drying out. Barley can be sown in winter or spring and modern barley varieties include Pearl and Optic. Some brewers swear by older types such as Maris Otter and Golden Promise but have to get them grown under contract at a high premium.

It is possible to malt other cereals and in combination with malted barley they will contribute different flavours: rye (spiciness), oats (smoothness) and wheat (thirst-quenching dryness). Wheat will also promote a beer's foam formation.

Barley arriving at the maltings will be sieved to remove any

Barley ripening in high Norfolk. This is a winter-sown variety called Pearl.

small corns or bits of stalk and dried to ensure it will keep until it is malted. The first stage of malting is 'steeping', which involves soaking the grain in water. Periodically the water will be drawn off and the barley 'air rested' to mimic conditions in the field. After two days and at over 40 per cent moisture the corns will start to show growth of roots. The barley is moved to a germination vessel in which humidified air is passed through the grain bed to provide oxygen for respiration and to keep the barley cool. The corns are turned to prevent the rootlets matting together, which would otherwise impede the vital airflow.

Germination needs three to four days as this is how long it takes to complete the activation of the enzymes before the 'green malt' can be heated in a kiln, gently at first to evaporate the water without destroying the important enzymes. As the moisture drops, air can be recirculated to save energy and the temperature increased to 'cure' the malt, producing colour and flavouring compounds. Kilning takes twenty-four to thirty-six hours. Lager malt has the palest colour while further kilning yields ale malts with darker colours and more intense malty flavours.

Speciality malts can be made by roasting pale malts in drums to produce amber, brown, chocolate and then black malt, depending on the temperature reached. For darker products, the drum needs to be quenched with cold water at just the right time to prevent the whole lot catching fire. Other flavoured

Malt is roasted in 1.5 tonne revolving drums. To produce black malt, a temperature of 210°C (410°F) is used and the drum has to be quenched with cold water at just the right moment to stop it catching fire! This drum is one of five at Thomas Fawcett in Castleford, West Yorkshire.

malts are produced by putting green malt into a drum and raising the temperature while the corns are still wet. The enzymes convert starch to sugars, which then caramelise. This process yields munich, carapils and crystal malts. Darker malts add colour to milds, porters and stouts, while the crystal family adds a chestnut colour to beer and a strong malty taste.

A batch of crystal malt being tested after roasting at Thomas Fawcett, Castleford.

Old floor maltings are low buildings with small windows and characteristic cowls on the kilns. This one was in use up to 1960 and in 2004 was being used as a store by Donnington Brewery near Stow-on-the-Wold in the Cotswolds.

The traditional view of a maltings is of a long low building with small windows and a distinctive cowl above the kilns at one end. Here the malt was produced on floors and was spread thinly to control the temperature and turned regularly by hand to keep the rootlets apart. The last floor malting was built in Grimsby, Lincolnshire, in 1952 and at the start of the twenty-first century only a handful are still in use. Floors have given way to pneumatic maltings, where the barley is germinated in much larger quantities in vessels with forced airflow and mechanical turners.

Turning the floor at Crisp's Great Ryburgh No. 19 Malthouse, which was built early in the twentieth century and still produces 2500 tonnes a year. The inset shows the rake that lifts and separates the corn to keep the 'piece' cool and stops the rootlets from matting.

In modern maltings the germination takes place in large slotted-bottomed vessels. This one at the Malting Company of Ireland plant in Cork is just being filled with a 'piece' of 160 tonnes – enough for six thousand barrels of beer or 120,000 bottles of whisky. The floor is turning below the static grain turner.

Malt provides the starch and the enzymes for the brewer to produce a fermentable sugar extract which he calls 'wort'. There is usually an excess of enzymes present, which allows unmalted cereal to be added to some beers, especially American lagers. However, maize and rice need boiling first to unravel the starch molecules ('gelatinisation'). Brewers can also adjust the fermentability of the wort by adding wheat or maize syrups with a whole host of different sugar spectra. In Britain a 10–20 per cent content of these syrups is not unusual.

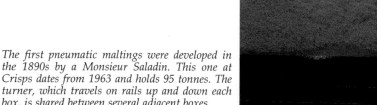

The first pneumatic maltings were developed in the 1890s by a Monsieur Saladin. This one at Crisps dates from 1963 and holds 95 tonnes. The turner, which travels on rails up and down each box, is shared between several adjacent boxes.

HOPS

A lot of people think that beer is made from hops. Indeed hops are used only in the brewing of beer but 100 litres of typical 4 per cent ABV (alcohol by volume) ale will use only 100 grams of hops, which is about a tenth of the weight of malt. Hops are better described as the 'spice' of beer. The hop is an odd plant; it has male and female flowers on separate plants and it is distantly related to the elm tree and to cannabis but without any of the latter's psychedelic properties.

The crop is bought on the concentration of an active bittering ingredient called 'alpha acid' (α acid). Traditional varieties such as Golding and Fuggles, which have been around since the nineteenth century, weigh in at around 4 per cent α acid. Plant breeding has increased yields, the greatest concentration being found in a variety called Admiral, which can contain 17 per cent. The hop cone is strictly not a flower but a strobilus formed of overlapping bracheoles. At the base of each bracheole, by the stem, yellow resinous lupulin glands contain the active bitter ingredient and the oils that give hops such a distinctive aroma.

Bitterness is extracted from the hops by boiling, during which process all of the aroma will go up the chimney. To retain hop aromas, some hops have to be added after the main boil in a process called 'late hopping' or else later still as 'dry hops' to the cask. Classic Pilsener lagers are late hopped, as are robust English ales.

Hops – 'the spice of beer' – ripening in the Herefordshire sun.

Every year hops grow from a rootstock to over 5 metres in height and are supported on expensive wood and wirework. The hopyard is strung in the autumn and the shoots trained up the strings every spring. At harvest time the strings are cut down and the 'hop-bines' taken to sheds, where the cones are separated from the leaves. Fresh hops need to be dried quickly to prevent deterioration. Even then hops are easily oxidised by the air if not kept cold until required. Many brewers use pelleted hops, which have been milled, compressed and vacuum-packed for ambient storage.

The oast-houses of Kent and Worcestershire with their conspicuous conical cowls are famous reminders of an industry that peaked at 29,053 hectares in fifty-three counties in 1878. Today the area is only around 1300 hectares in six counties as beers have lower bitterness levels, the yield of α acid has improved and continental lagers brewed in Britain often use imported hops from Germany and the United States. In the old days picking needed vast amounts of labour and so the industry consolidated in areas close to large centres of population – near London and the West Midlands.

Hops grown on high wires are cut down and moved to a picking shed (above). Beaters will remove the leaves and cones and a series of shakers will separate the heavier cones from the leaves (below).

Oasts are no longer brick towers with conical cowls. This one at Claston in Herefordshire was built in 2002. Sensors above the bed of cones control the gas burners and the recycling of warm air.

In modern times each hectare of hop garden will yield 1.5 to 1.8 tonnes of hops. Plant breeding has centred on hedgerow varieties that grow to around 2.5 metres tall. The breeders have reduced the internodal distance (the space between points at which leaves branch from the growing stem) to get the same number of cones from a much shorter plant. The attraction is lower-cost support for the crop and machine picking rather than carrying the bines off to picking sheds, which demand high levels of casual labour. Hedgerow varieties accounted for a fifth of the English crop in 2003.

WATER

Beer is well over 90 per cent water and a modern brewery uses from four to seven units of water for every unit of beer

Most breweries had their own supply of well water. This is the shallow well at the Brunswick microbrewery in Derby. The water is used only for cooling as its quality cannot be guaranteed in the twenty-first century.

Coors in Burton upon Trent uses a deep bore supply from over 120 metres (394 feet) below ground to ensure a consistent analysis and no pollution from the twenty-first century above. Water is seen cascading into a tank at the top of the company's 1866 water-tower.

sold. Brewers call water 'liquor' and, when they had wooden casks to clean, twice as much would have been used. Water supplies dictated where brewing industries became established. Good-quality water led to good-quality beer that could be sold well away from where it was brewed. Beer from Burton upon Trent, Staffordshire, was known in London in the 1620s when an overland journey would have been long and expensive. Burton water is high in dissolved gypsum (calcium sulphate). The calcium increases the acidity of the mash of malt and water slightly, which ensures that the starch-breaking enzymes work more effectively. In turn the beer has a lower pH value and is less prone to infection, thus extending its shelf life for more distant sale. Indeed the highly hopped East India pale ales matured nicely on their long trip around the Cape of Good Hope, crossing the equator twice on the journey to Calcutta.

As well as altering the chemistry in the mash tun, the dissolved ions in water can contribute directly to flavour: iron from sandstone sources will give an unacceptable 'inky' flavour, while on the positive side sulphate gives a crisp dryness and chloride a round fullness. Mild ales have more chloride, bitters more sulphate.

In the nineteenth century London brewers Ind Coope, Truman, Mann and Charrington opened breweries in Burton to allow them to enter the growing market for pale ales, since London water was more suitable to brewing darker, fuller-flavoured beers. Up to the 1950s the Bolton brewer Magee Marshall transported water in special rail tankers from its own Burton well. Eventually scientists learned how to treat water with added salts to match that from any other location in a process still known as 'burtonisation'. More delicately flavoured lagers use waters with much lower levels of dissolved salts – the classic water from Pilsen (Plzen) in the Czech Republic, where the first pale lager was brewed in the 1840s, is very soft indeed.

PROCESSING AIDS

Malt, hops and water are the main ingredients, with added maize or wheat syrups. Brewers do add small amounts of other materials to tune the process. With no requirement to list ingredients on beers in Britain, it is perhaps instructive to look at the following list and wonder whether some of them could be dispensed with if they had to be declared. We have already mentioned the addition of salts to water. Enzymes produced from fungal fermentations can be added to the mash to ensure

How strong is beer?

The strength of alcoholic beverages is measured according to the percentage of alcohol by volume (ABV) (millilitres of ethanol per 100 ml). Spirits are 40 per cent, sherry around 18 per cent, table wines 10–12 per cent, but with the long tradition of low-strength thirst-quenching beer for manual labourers the average ABV percentage of British beers is only 4.2. In Europe the average is nearer 5.0 per cent.

The average covers a wide range, from Mann's Brown at 2.8 per cent, standard beers at up to 4.5 per cent, premium continental lagers at around 5.0 per cent to barley wines at 10 per cent. Europe's strongest lager is Samiclaus from Austria at 14 per cent but the world record is Sam Adams Utopias from Boston in the United States, which weighs in at a massive 25 per cent. Aimed directly at the after-dinner liqueur market, this limited-edition beer came in a bottle shaped like a brewing kettle and has fetched several hundreds of dollars in Internet auctions.

that all the barley gums are broken down. Modern rapid malting can leave gums intact, which will impede filtration and can form hazes. Enzymes can also be added to make 'lite' beers by converting some normally unfermentable sugars to fermentable ones. Antifoam is added to keep the fermenting beer in the vessel, while the addition of small amounts of zinc or copper sulphate ensures the yeast is not short of vital minerals that were once dissolved naturally from soldered copper equipment. Some brewers add yeast food to ensure that the fermentation gets off to a rapid start.

Antioxidants (ascorbic acid and sulphur dioxide) are useful in scavenging undesirable oxygen molecules that might otherwise lead

to stale flavours and beer hazes. There are a host of processing aids designed to prevent hazes in beer. Isinglass finings will precipitate yeast from suspension; seaweed preparations will precipitate protein, as will extracts of acidified silicates and acacia gum. Protein of specific molecular size can be adsorbed by filtering beer through silica hydrogel, and haze-forming tannins by passage through a synthetic insoluble protein called poly vinyl polypyrrolidone (PVPP for short). With the presentation of beer in the glass being so important, the addition of propylene glycol alginate (E405) can assist the head (foam) retention.

Brewers go to great lengths to ensure bright worts and beers at every stage of the process. These samples are at Arkells in Swindon.

The brewing process

MASHING

Malt needs to be crushed to allow hot water to wet the malt quickly and get the enzymes working to convert the starch into sugars. The fineness of the grind is dictated by the method used to separate the sugar solution (wort) from the spent grain. A mash tun needs a coarse grind in order to keep the husk as integral as possible because it will be used as a filter bed. In a mash filter, where the filtration medium is a polypropylene cloth, the milling can be much finer. Traditional mills have two or three pairs of rollers, sometimes with internal sieves to provide a consistent particle-size spectrum, which guarantees good conversion to sugar and efficient filtration.

In the past ground malt (grist) was tipped into a mash tun full of hot water and the mash was mixed with wooden paddles by hand. The malt enzymes produced a sugar solution (wort), which was drained off through a slotted false bottom. The grain was re-wetted with a second 'water', mixed and run off again, followed by a third water. Gradually manual mash mixing was

Left: The mill at Hook Norton dates from 1899. A belt-driven sieve separates the malt into big and small corns, which are directed to rollers set at different gaps. It may be a fire hazard, but three of the brewery workers are part-time firemen!

Right: This Porteus mill at Okells on the Isle of Man has two gaps. The top rollers crack the corns, and between the sets of rollers are sieves to divert the husk and flour past the second set, which further crushes the larger 'grits'. Grind consistency is key to a good extract, so it will be checked daily by sieving samples.

The mash tun is heated with hot water before mashing. The Steels masher behind will mix the grist with hot water after the trumpet (top right) has been lowered into position.

replaced with mechanised mash-tun rakes and later the Steels mashing machine. This is a series of screws and tines in a cylindrical tube that ensures a good mix before the mash enters the tun. The temperature of a mash is around 65°C (149°F) and the enzymes take about sixty to ninety minutes to complete their work before wort run-off is started.

The successive mashes have been replaced by 'sparging', which involves hot water being sprayed on to the top of the mash bed from a rotating arm. Water is sprayed at the same rate as the wort is run off to ensure that the grain does not blind the slots in the plates. It takes up to three hours to recover all the sugar. The spent grain is removed and sold as cattle feed.

The process of mash conversion and run-off in a single vessel means that a mash is possible only every eight hours. The 'unit operations' of mash conversion (enzymic breakdown of the starch) and run-off can be separated into two vessels – a mash

To leach all the sugar from the mash, 'sparge liquor' is applied, using a revolving arm. This one is at the Beer Station microbrewery in Horsham, Sussex.

This 8.8 metre (29 foot) diameter lauter tun was built by Huppman for SAB Miller in Poland. In Germany, where the Purity Laws prohibit additions, the shoes at the base of the knives can be made of a zinc-rich alloy to dissolve a tiny amount of this essential ion into the wort. Yeast needs zinc to ferment satisfactorily.

mixer combined with a lauter tun or mash filter. The mash mixer is a stirred vessel in which the enzymic conversion takes place and the mash can be heated to over 75°C (167°F) to reduce the viscosity just before transfer for separation.

The lauter tun also has a slotted bottom but the grain depth will be 35–45 cm (up to 18 inches) rather than 1.2 metres as in

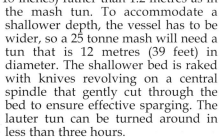

the mash tun. To accommodate a shallower depth, the vessel has to be wider, so a 25 tonne mash will need a tun that is 12 metres (39 feet) in diameter. The shallower bed is raked with knives revolving on a central spindle that gently cut through the bed to ensure effective sparging. The lauter tun can be turned around in less than three hours.

The mash filter has a bank of frames, each fitted with an inflatable diaphragm. Mash is filtered through cloths and bright wort is collected. Gently inflating the diaphragms will push the mash against the cloth. As the 'squeeze' is relaxed, sparge water will flood into the gap ready for a second squeeze to leach out the remaining sugar. A very shallow grain depth ensures rapid run-off with excellent extract recovery, so the filter easily yields twelve brews a day.

A modern mash filter at Interbrew's plant in Glasgow. Filtration through a polypropylene cloth rather than metal slots gives improved recovery of sugar extract.

Adding hops to the copper at Adnams in Southwold. More modern plants will use chutes for addition to avoid having to turn the steam off.

BOILING

Wort is boiled with hops in coppers or 'kettles' (as they are usually made of stainless steel these days). Look carefully at copper vessels today and you will probably see that they are shrouds disguising stainless-steel interiors. The heating surfaces are steam pipes that direct the wort upwards into an inverted cone topped with a spreader, which directs boiling wort back into the liquid to create a rolling boil. Good agitation extracts the bitterness from the hops and aids the precipitation of unwanted protein, which might cause later haze in the beer. Boiling will take from forty-five to ninety minutes. Copper finings derived from seaweeds are added right at the end of the boil to precipitate more protein ('trub') and late hops will be added at the same time.

Above: *The steam-heating element inside this copper calandria at Arkells in Swindon forces the boiling wort up to the spreader, which directs it back down into the wort to get a rolling boil.*

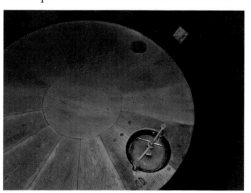

A hop-back has a slotted bottom like the mash tun to allow the wort to drain through. The hops are removed by manually finding the plug beneath a metre (3 feet) of hops, then shovelling them down the hole. This is thirsty work but Health and Safety rules dictate that no beer may be consumed in a modern plant.

The other 92 per cent of British beer is 'brewery conditioned' – that is, prepared for dispensing in the brewery and put into containers that need no further treatment before drinking. After fermentation yeast will be completely removed by centrifugation and the beer chilled in tanks to $-1^{\circ}C$ ($30^{\circ}F$). This temperature encourages hazes to form by the precipitation of protein and tannins that originate from the malt and the hops. British brewers generally add isinglass finings in the maturation tank to aid the settling of the haze material.

There is an increasing tendency for beers to be served cooler, with some ales being sold at $6^{\circ}C$ ($43^{\circ}F$), and there is even a lager from Coors called Arc that has ice floating in it! It is vital that beer remains bright at low temperatures, so the brewer will aim to remove more protein and tannin from the solution by the use of processing aids.

Beer is filtered using a kieselguhr powder to trap any yeasts and other particulate matter. The carbon dioxide and nitrogen will be adjusted in pressure-controlled injection loops. Processing economies ensue from brewing, fermenting and maturing at 6–7 per cent ABV and diluting with de-aerated water before packaging. Micro-organisms are destroyed by heat pasteurisation either before packaging (for kegs) or after (for bottles and cans). As this is a very energy-intensive process many brewers are turning to sterile filtration through plastic membranes to reduce costs and produce a fresher-tasting beer, especially towards the end of its shelf life.

PACKAGING

Just over half of British beer is filled into kegs. The bright beer in the pub is pushed to the bar using gas pressure and pumps. Kegs are washed and filled with bright pasteurised beer.

Smallpack beers come in bottles (12 per cent of the market) and cans (27 per cent). There are few returnable bottles these days. The incoming empties are rinsed and air is evacuated from the containers using carbon dioxide flushes before filling under pressure. The can end or bottle crown is applied, ensuring that no oxygen gets in. Oxygen is the enemy

Richard White filling casks on Hall & Woodhouse's modern line at Blandford Forum in Dorset.

of brewery-conditioned beer as it encourages the formation of stale flavours and increases haze levels.

Developments in beer packaging include lightweight bottles and narrower can ends that use less expensive aluminium. Plastic bottles offer big economies in transport as they are less than half the weight of glass but barrier technology has only just become good enough to guarantee that carbon dioxide will not get out and that oxygen will not get in to stale the product. Beer in plastic is sold at events at which ebullient behaviour may risk the empties being used as missiles but the wider market has yet to accept them. Carlsberg uses returnable plastic bottles in Denmark and Bitburger beer from Germany is available in plastic screw-top bottles in British supermarkets, so the market looks set to grow.

Nitrogen technology has been applied to canned beer and even to bottled Guinness. Different technologies put liquid nitrogen directly into the 'widget' or add a few drops before closing the container. When the can is opened, the change in pressure creates a fine jet of beer and gas from the device, encouraging the formation of a thick creamy head.

This microbrewery at Moorhouses in Burnley, Lancashire, dates from 1988 but the layout is typical of many of today's smaller breweries. The mash tun and the grain elevator are on the left. The hidden vessel in the middle is a redundant whirlpool, as the copper on the right is now fitted with a sieve to hold back the spent hops and trub. The blue blocks on the staging in front of the copper are invert sugar waiting addition.

Wort movement is by water power at the Donnington Brewery in the Cotswolds. The inset shows the belt-driven pump, which moves wort upstairs to the copper.

The romance of beer

EARLY HISTORY

Early clay tablets record the brewers of the Sumer civilisation almost six thousand years ago. Long before that someone must have wetted some grain to initiate growth, somehow more water was added and wild yeasts in the air fermented the resulting mush.

Modern researchers have tried to mimic the first brewers by baking loaves of barley bread and then mashing them. Malting takes place up to 20°C, fermentation up to 30°C, starch conversion up to 70°C, but gelatinisation of maize or millet requires even higher temperatures. It remains unclear how the first brewers managed these temperature requirements as baking would gelatinise the starch but destroy the starch-breaking

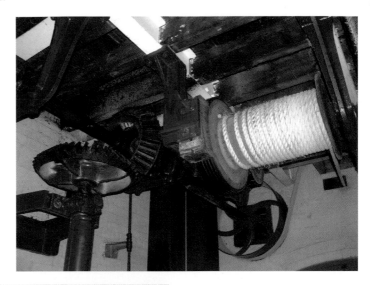

The malt-sack hoist at Hook Norton is belt-driven by a 25 horsepower steam engine.

Brewing was a domestic pursuit for centuries. This frontispiece from Bailey's 'Household Management' of 1736 shows the lady of the house brewing.

enzymes. Fermentation is the easy bit as ancient people would have noticed the effect of leaving honey or fruit residues in the open for any length of time.

Perhaps there are clues in modern native African brewing, which employs a two-stage process: one stage gelatinises the corn and unwinds the starch molecules; the other produces the enzymes. Firstly raw millet is mixed to a stiff dough and buried underground for a week inside a plastic bag. This makes the dough very acidic. The dough is dried over an open fire and this gelatinises the starch. Meanwhile another batch of millet is

The photographs on this page illustrate brewing at a village in Uganda in the twenty-first century.
Left: Malted millet is spread on sheeting to dry in the sun.

A small mash of malted millet and acidified/gelatinised millet, the wort will be separated by squeezing from a woven sack.

Right: *Deo Lule, a brewer from the modern Uganda Breweries, samples the finished 'ajon' traditional beer.*

Left: *The village menfolk consume the 'ajon' through straws from a communal vessel.*

malted and sun-dried. If the dried gelatinised millet (four parts) is crushed with malted millet (one part) and water (six parts) is added, sugars will be produced that are fermented by yeast from the air. The effect of the earlier acidification ensures that most bacteria will be kept at bay. The resulting beer is drunk communally through straws from a large bucket in a very similar manner to that shown on some Sumer clay tablets in the British Museum.

It is clear from surviving records that beer played a major part in ancient life in Egypt and Mesopotamia. An early quality-control measure in Babylon involved the brewer of a substandard product being drowned in it! Archaeo-botanists have found residues in tomb excavations to suggest that honey, dates and juniper were mixed together with malted grains for the afterlife. Even where there are no written records, as on the Orkney Islands, pots will yield their secrets. A Skara Brae 'beer' from the Orkneys contained deadly nightshade, henbane and hemlock as well as malted grain – clearly designed to induce a trance during early rituals rather than to refresh and relax our ancestors!

Writing in the first century, Pliny observed that the tribes of northern Europe drank an intoxicating drink made from corn steeped in water. Tacitus declared a liking for wine and said that 'horrible' beer was the normal drink of the Germanic and Gallic tribes. *Atrectus ceruesarius* (Atrectus the brewer) was Britain's first known brewer, named on a wooden leaf tablet from the *Vindolanda* fort on Hadrian's Wall, dating from the second century. Viking burials have revealed a wheat brew flavoured with bilberries, cranberries and myrtle to help the warrior with his roistering in Valhalla.

BEER IN THE MIDDLE AGES

An early challenge was to balance the cloying fullness of strong ales with something more bitter. Bilberries and cranberries helped by giving acidity but were still themselves too sweet. The early bitter additions comprised *bouquet garnis* of various herbs called 'gruit', which was bog myrtle sometimes supplemented with rosemary and yarrow. As

Some old open vessels survive today. (Above) This open copper is at Wadworth in Devizes. (Left) This wooden fermenting square at Arkells in Swindon has been lined with copper.

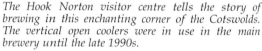

The Hook Norton visitor centre tells the story of brewing in this enchanting corner of the Cotswolds. The vertical open coolers were in use in the main brewery until the late 1990s.

Bridge of Allan, Stirling, Scotland (telephone: 01786 834555; website: www.bridgeofallan.co.uk) and **Hilden** in Northern Ireland (028 9266 3863). If you are near **Ridley's** brewery in Chelmsford (telephone: 01371 820316; website: www.ridleys.co.uk) on a summer Wednesday you can have a tour around. You can pre-book a tour of the **Chiltern Brewery** near Aylesbury (telephone: 01296 613647; website: www.chilternbrewery.co.uk). As well as beer, Chiltern has Britain's largest range of beer 'condiments'. Mustard, sausages, bread, cheese, shampoo and fruit cake are souped with their beers but there is also chocolate fudge with crystal malt, marmalade with dark malt extract, pickled eggs in hop vinegar and a 'gentleman's hop cologne'. The **Chiltern Valley Brewery** at Hambleden near Henley-on-Thames (telephone: 01491 638330; website: www.chilternvalley.co.uk) is attached to Old Luxters Vineyard but tours need to be pre-booked. **Elgoods** in Wisbech admits visitors to its brewery and adjoining gardens midweek during the summer (telephone: 01945 583160; website: www.elgoods-brewery.co.uk); the gardens have one of Britain's biggest *Gingko biloba* trees. As the tourist industry is in constant change, it is always best to contact the brewery before travelling and to keep an eye out for flyers in information offices.

You can visit one of Britain's last surviving floor maltings at **Tuckers** in Newton Abbot (telephone: 01626 334734; website: www.tuckersmaltings.com), which has a beer shop selling the produce of some of the thirty brewers supplied by the company.

Most microbreweries will gladly sell you a polypin of their cask beers if you knock on the door and will probably give you a quick look around as well.

Shire horses can be seen at Burton upon Trent, Hook Norton, Youngs in Wandsworth, **Robinsons** at Stockport (telephone: 0161 612 4061; website: www.frederic-robinson.co.uk), **Thwaites** in Blackburn (telephone: 01254 686868) and **Wadworth** in Devizes (telephone: 01380 723361; website: www.wadworth.co.uk). **Samuel Smiths** at Tadcaster (telephone: 01937 832225) stables its horses in York for

Inside the visitor centre at the St Austell Brewery in Cornwall.

making deliveries during the tourist season.

Little beer is sold in wooden casks these days but, while coopering memorabilia abounds, coopers are much rarer; they can be seen at Burton upon Trent and at Theakstons in Masham.

Steam engines are preserved *in situ* at Arkells, Holts, Shepherd Neame and Hall & Woodhouse. The one at Wadworth is still coupled to the steam supply for demonstration while Hook Norton brewing is still driven by an 1899 engine that cost £175.

Further afield masses of tourists flock to visitor centres at Heineken in Amsterdam, Carlsberg in Copenhagen and Anheuser Busch in St Louis. The massive £35 million Guinness Storehouse in Dublin is Ireland's biggest tourist attraction with over two million visitors every year. It is not just Munich that has its *Oktoberfest*; there is a large tent set up beside most Bavarian breweries every autumn for a celebration of lager (without a glass of wine or an alcopop in sight) enjoyed to the strains of an ebullient oompah band. Each June the Staropramen brewery in Prague attracts twenty thousand people to an open day. The whole of the town of Shiner in Texas turned out to sample a new beer produced by the tiny Spoetzl brewery. Why is it that a mere few dozen people watch the International Barrel Rolling Championships in Burton upon Trent, yet the Czech heat is watched by seven thousand? Perhaps one day the British will take more of an interest in their national drink.

Bars for visitors are usually full of memorabilia. This one at Okells on the Isle of Man has a bar made from the body and top of an old vessel.

Further reading

Michael Jackson's *World Guide to Beer* (Michael Jackson, 1988) and Brian Glover's *World Encyclopedia of Beer* (Anness Publishing, 1999) cover the general history of brewing and explore the beers of the world. *Michael Jackson's Pocket Beer Book* (Mitchell Beazley, 1997) packs most of the information into a small volume but without illustrations. Roger Protz fills almost two hundred pages of *The Complete Encyclopedia of Wine, Beer and Spirits* (Carlton, 2000) with a very similar scope.

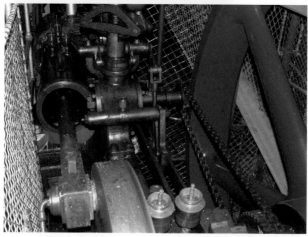

Old steam engines are still found in breweries. These examples at Blandford Forum (left) and Swindon no longer work for their living.

Protz's *The Taste of Beer: A Guide to Appreciating the Great Beers of the World* (Weidenfeld & Nicolson, 1998) and his *Ale Trail* (Eric Dobby, 1995) have loads of good illustrations. The well-researched *Beer: The Story of the Pint* by Martyn Cornell (Headline, 2003) covers the British industry and debunks a few myths on the way. The definitive economic stories of British brewing are Peter Mathias's *The Brewing Industry in England 1700–1830* (Cambridge University Press, 1959) and Gourvish and Wilson's *History of the British Brewing Industry 1830–1980* (Cambridge University Press, 1994) – but a lot has happened since 1980. To keep abreast of the ever-shifting list of smaller brewers, the annual *Good Beer Guide* edited by Jeff Evans (CAMRA) is a must. The Association of Brewers in the United States has a series of books devoted to different beer styles, while CAMRA's *Homebrew Classics* series, while aiming to downsize commercial recipes from today and yesteryear, does present a wealth of interesting historical points. If you are interested in what does go and has gone into beer, try Jeffrey Patton's *Additives in Beer* (Patton, 1989). On the subject of beer and food, the head brewer at the Brooklyn Brewery in New York, Garrett Oliver, has some great ideas in *The Brewmaster's Table* (HarperCollins, 2003), although the book uses some specifically American cooking terms. The Beer Education Trust (Beer Academy) started educational courses in 2004; for up-to-date details consult their website (www.beeracademy.org). For an up-to-date synopsis of the state of the British industry you can download the Interbrew Market Report from the Interbrew website (www.interbrew.com).

The old and the new. This rare 'swinging Valentine' (left) at Arkells in Swindon controls the flow of wort from the mash tun to avoid sucking the grain bed down on to the slotted bottom. Britain's most modern beer-bottling line (right) was commissioned at Scottish Courage in Tadcaster during July 2004.

Some British beers to try

Unashamedly the choice is the author's. There are obviously many fine beers brewed up and down the land that he has yet to try, so he humbly apologises to the brewers who are not mentioned. Lager is fine on a sunny day: a glass of German lager slips down a treat on a visit to the Fatherland – even Spanish lager refreshes the parts before a poolside siesta. This list aims to direct readers to beers with a British heritage that are well worth tasting. See what you think…

ON DRAUGHT – SORRY, NO KEGS HERE!

Adnams Bitter: a yummy quaffable beer, well worth the trip to Southwold on the Suffolk coast. Quite high bitterness (35 bitterness units) for a 3.7 per cent ABV beer but has a great hoppy nose. If you are there in the winter, try Fisherman.

Bathams Best Bitter : just proves the Black Country is not all about milds.

Brakspears Bitter: like Hook Norton Bitter, this 3.4 per cent ABV beer is fighting way beyond its lowish alcohol content with a high fermentable residue and lots of hop bitterness. Production has returned to Oxfordshire, where Wychwood have installed the old 'dropping system', as originally used at its Henley home.

Camerons Strongarm: a chestnut bitter with a lot of crystal malt and a big head.

Elgood's Black Dog: 3.6 per cent ABV, a traditional dark mild with some splendid roasted, bitter flavours. This brewery is unusual in producing more dark beers than light.

Highgate Mild: the very best dark mild, oozing with malty roast flavours.

Hook Norton Bitter: lovely pale beer with a nice hop. Has a low ABV percentage so try lots of it in the pub garden in the sunshine.

Interbrew Draught Bass: still going strong, still brewed by Coors in Burton, still as nutty as it was.

Jennings Bitter: one of the maltiest bitters around. One of my firm favourites. It is still made using solid blocks of tasty invert sugar.

Marstons Pedigree: the only beer still brewed in Burton Unions this side of Firestone Walker in California, where they use casks only a third the size of the traditional Burton ones. All Maris Otter malt, floor malted at their own Lichfield maltings. Fruity, spicy and dry all at the same time – a truly superb beer.

Moorhouses Pride of Pendle: a very moreish beer (4.1 per cent ABV) with just the right balance of maltiness, fullness and hops. Brewed with the finest ingredients, late-hopped with Fuggles and Willamette, with only a microscope and a pH meter to assist the brewer.

Orkney Red MacGregor: from a tiny brewery that uses American dry hops imaginatively.

St Austell Tribute: a nirvanic cross between Jennings Bitter and Timothy Taylor's Landlord with carapils, munich and wheat malts and Willamette late hops.

Timothy Taylor Landlord: expensive Golden Promise malt and Whitbread Goldings Variety hops, this little brewery cuts no corners. Even Madonna likes this one!

Wadworth JCB: not named after a digger but the founder, J. C. Bartholomew. Contains plenty of crystal malt. 25 per cent of the hops are added after boiling as a 'tea'.

IN BOTTLE

Arran Blond: once a wheat beer, but the label no longer mentions that. The delightful hop aroma is still there.

Badger Blandford Fly: delicate cinnamon and ginger flavours – very subtle.

Bateman's XXXB: a fine Lincolnshire bitter in bottle. Note the unique bottle-neck design.

Black Sheep Riggwelter: from an old Norse word meaning a sheep that is on its back and cannot right itself without help. This well-crafted dark ale is still brewed in Yorkshire stone squares and has delicious chocolate malt notes.

Cains Dragonheart: a surviving Lancashire brown ale with a rich and roasted flavour.

Caledonian Deuchars IPA: the bottled version of a champion British cask beer. Very pale and hoppy.

Caledonian Edinburgh Strong: just what you need on a cold night in the Scottish capital. 6.4 per cent ABV with oodles of treacly notes.

Davenports Top Brew de Luxe: a Brum revival now brewed at Highgate. Davenports used to deliver direct to your door. It really packs a punch above its 7.2 per cent ABV.

Gales Prize Old Ale: you will need a corkscrew to open this one. A rich ruby colour, powerful aroma and very warming – the archetypal barley wine. Just right with a plate of robust English cheeses.

Greene King Strong Suffolk: a rare survivor of what beer might once have tasted like. A 12 per cent ABV brew that has been matured for two years in wooden vats is blended with a newer beer; the resulting 6 per cent ABV dark beer has a subtle acidic twang just like old porter.

Harveys Imperial Extra Double Stout: this 9 per cent ABV beer is in a corked bottle. Its flavours are even longer than its brand name.

Harviestoun Bitter and Twisted: oozing with citrusy hops, this beer actually smells of grapefruit. CAMRA Champion Beer in cask in 2003, the bottled version is more widely available and won a trophy at the 2004 Brewing Awards for the best bottled ale.

Hogsback TEA: a beautiful hoppy beer in one of the best-badged bottles I've seen. Gold and green, great presentation.

Hopback Summer Lightning: *the* summer refresher.

Innis & Gunn Oak Aged Beer: this 6.6 per cent ABV Scottish ale is matured in new American oak casks for a precise seventy-seven days. Interesting – it really does taste like the inside of a cask! Vanilla and cigar-box aromas on wines have nothing on Innis & Gunn.

J. W. Lees Harvest Ale: brewed each autumn from the latest harvest of Maris Otter barley and East Kent Golding hops. At 11.5 per cent ABV, this beer needs treating with respect. Pale in colour, it has a warm, estery aroma and a long dry finish which goes well with Stilton cheese.

Marstons Old Empire: the beer that made Burton famous. Not quite as strong and less bitter but very tasty nonetheless.

Wychwood Circle Master: the best organic ale on the British market. It even uses old high-growing Plumage Archer barley. This barley finds its way into the Prince of Wales's Duchy Original organic ale, also brewed at Wychwood.

Youngs Double Chocolate Stout: really luscious – they do put real chocolate in the copper.

Index

ABV (alcohol by volume)
17, 26
Acacia gum 17
Ajon (Uganda native beer)
30
Ale 22, 33, 39
Ale conners 32
Allsopp, Samuel 35, 36
Anheuser Busch 47, 51
Antioxidants 17
Atrectus 31
Babylon 31
Barley 8
Barley varieties 8, 54
Bavaria 24
Beer Academy 45, 53
Beer and food 45
Beer and health 44
Beer image 7, 44
Beer Orders 1989 41
Beer statistics 6, 7, 14, 26
Beer styles 39
Bitterness 13, 21, 31
Bohemia 33, 39
Boiling 21
Brewery conditioning 26
Burton Unions 23
Burton upon Trent 16, 22,
32, 36, 50, 51, 55
Burtonisation 16
CAMRA (Campaign for
Real Ale) 55
Carbon dioxide 23, 24, 26,
27
Carlsberg 27, 39, 42, 46, 51
Cask beer 4, 8, 50
Cellar 25
Cereals 8
Coors 4, 16, 26, 41, 42, 46,
49, 54
Copper (kettle) 21
Czech Republic 16, 51
Dreher, Anton 39
Egypt 31
Enzymes 8, 9, 10, 16, 17, 18,
19, 29
Esters 24
Exports 7

Fermentation 22, 33
Filtration 26
Firkin 33
Floor malting 11, 50
Gelatinisation 12, 28, 29, 30
George III 34
Germination 9, 33
Glucose 8, 23
Grist 18
Gruit 31
Guinness 27, 37, 46, 51
Hansen, Emil 39, 49
Haze 8, 17, 21, 26, 27
Hedgerow hops 15
High gravity brewing 26
Hildegarde of Bingen 33
Hop varieties 24, 54
Hops 13, 21, 24, 33
Imports 7
Interbrew 42, 46, 53, 54
Ions 16
IPA (India Pale Ale) 16, 36,
55
Isinglass finings 17, 24, 25
Jacobsen, Christian 39
Kieselguhr 26
Kilderkin 33
Kilning 9
Lager 22, 24, 39, 54
Lambic beer 23
Lauter tun 20
Lite beers 17
Malt, crystal 10, 54
Malt, dark 9
Malting 8
Mash filter 18, 20
Mash mixer 20
Mash tun 16, 19
Mashing 18
Mesopotamia 31
Millet 29
Milling 18
Monasteries 32, 34
Munich 38, 51
Nitrogen 24, 25, 26, 27
Nitrokeg 25
Oxygen 9, 17, 22, 26,
Packaging 26

Pasteur, Louis 24
Pasteurisation 26
PGA (Propylene glycol
alginate) 17
Pilsener 13, 38, 39
Plastic bottles 27
Porter 34, 35
Processing aids 16
Protein 8, 17, 21, 25, 32
Pubs 42
PVPP (poly vinyl
polypyrrolidone) 17
Reinheitsgobot (German
Purity Law) 8, 20
Scottish & Newcastle 41, 42,
46
Seaweed 17
Sedlmeyer, Gabriel 38
Silica hydrogel 17
Silicates 17
Sparging 19, 20
Speciality malts 9
Spent grains 19
Spontaneous fermentation
23, 29, 30
Steel's masher 19
Steeping 9
Supermarkets 6, 27, 43
Tacitus 31
Tax 7, 32
Tesco Beer Challenge 6
Trub 21
Vindolanda 31
Visitor centres 49
Volume measurement 7
Water 16
Weihenstephan 32
Wenceslas 33
Whirlpool 22
Whitbread, Samuel 34
Widget 27
William IV 37
Wort 12, 18, 19, 22
Worthington, William 35
Yeast 4, 23, 25
Yeast culture collection 24
Zinc 17